# FRENCH SONGS
## for *Accordion*

Arranged by
GARY MEISNER

ISBN 978-1-4234-3590-7

HAL•LEONARD®
CORPORATION

7777 W. BLUEMOUND RD. P.O. BOX 13819 MILWAUKEE, WI 53213

Visit Hal Leonard Online at
**www.halleonard.com**

# CONTENTS

# AUTUMN LEAVES

English lyric by JOHNNY MERCER
French lyric by JACQUES PREVERT
Music by JOSEPH KOSMA

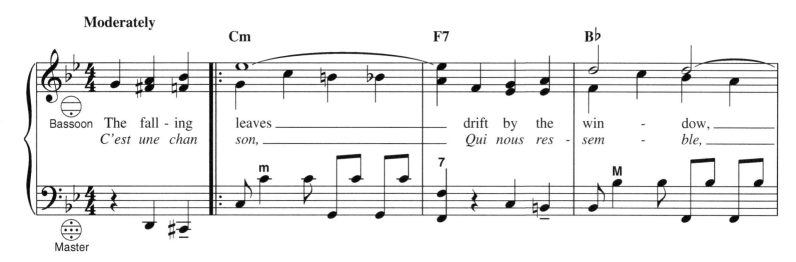

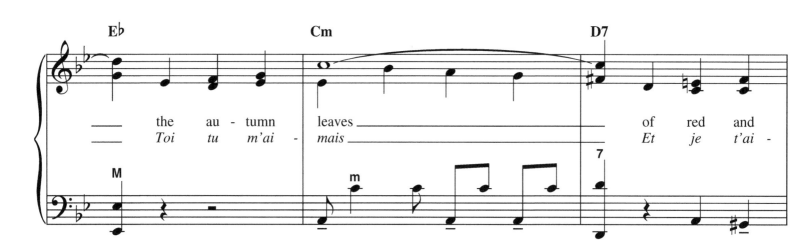

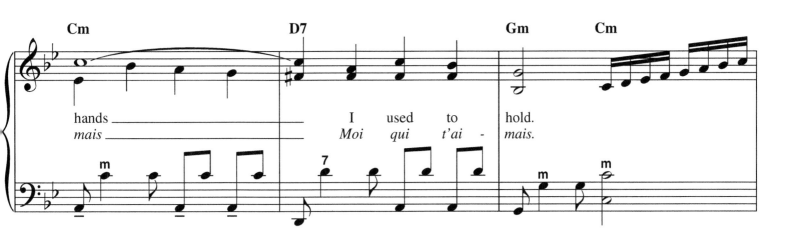

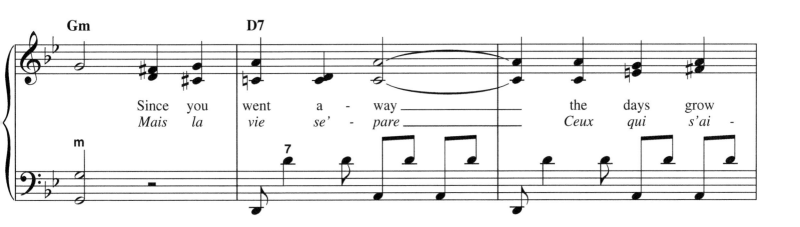

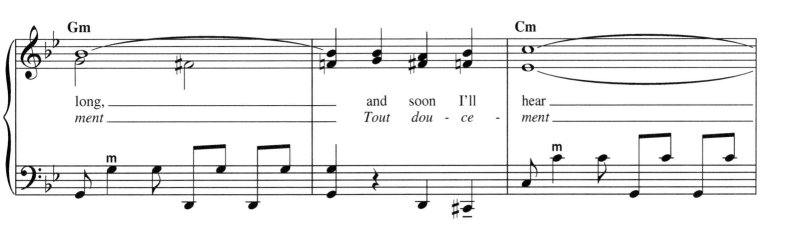

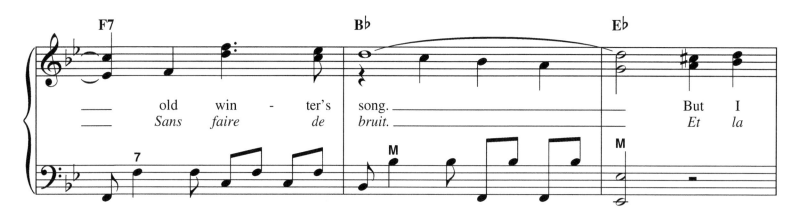

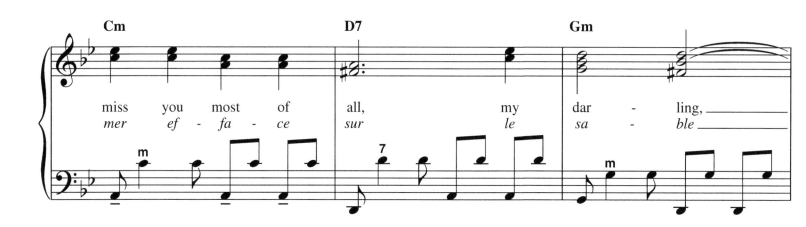

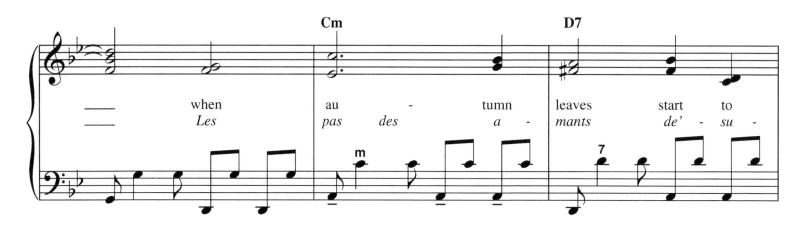

# C'EST MAGNIFIQUE
## from CAN-CAN

Words and Music by
COLE PORTER

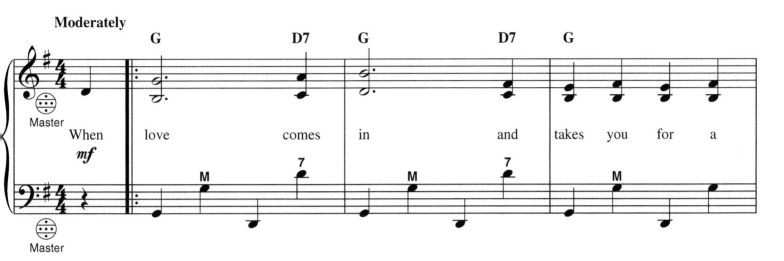

When love comes in and takes you for a

spin, oo la la-la,⎯ c'est mag - ni -

fi - que. When ev - 'ry

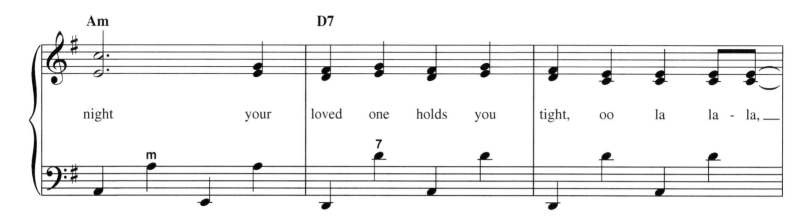

night　　　　　your　loved　one　holds　you　　tight,　oo　la　la - la, ___

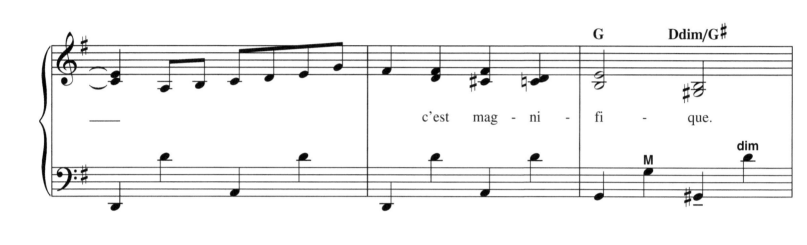

___　　　　　　　　　　　　　　　c'est　mag - ni - fi - que.

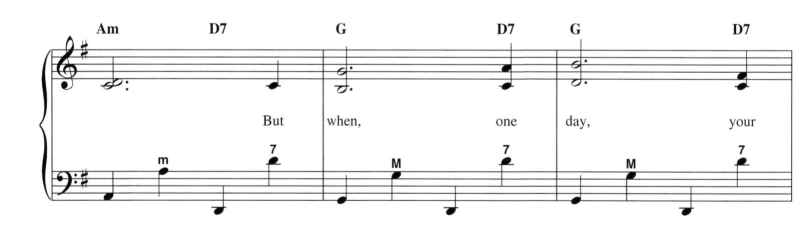

But　when,　　　　one　day,　　　your

loved　one　drifts　a - way,　oo　la　la-la, ___

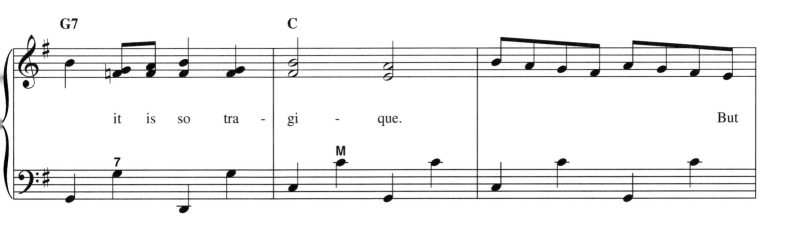

it is so tra - gi - que. But

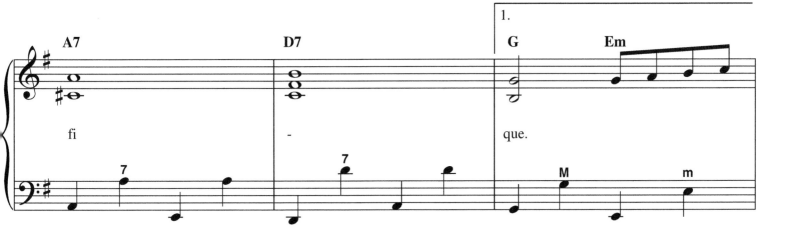

when, once more, { he } { she } whis - pers "je t'a - dore" c'est mag - ni -

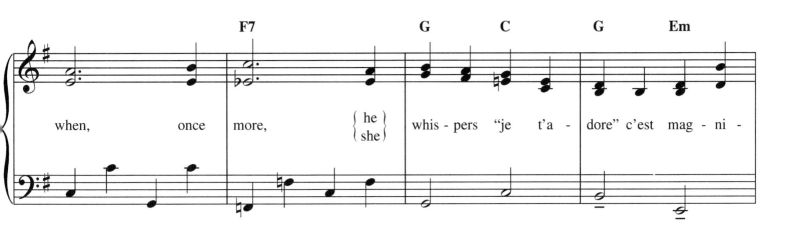

1.

fi - que.

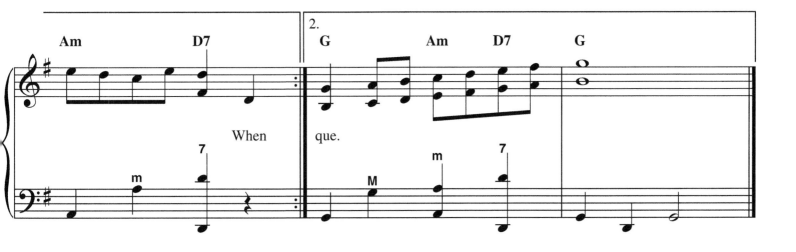

2.

When que.

# BEYOND THE SEA

By ALBERT LASRY and CHARLES TRENET
English Lyrics by JACK LAWRENCE

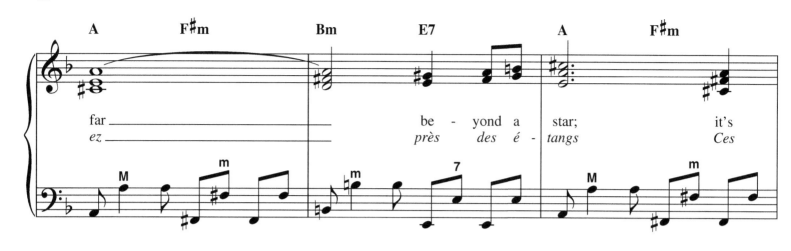

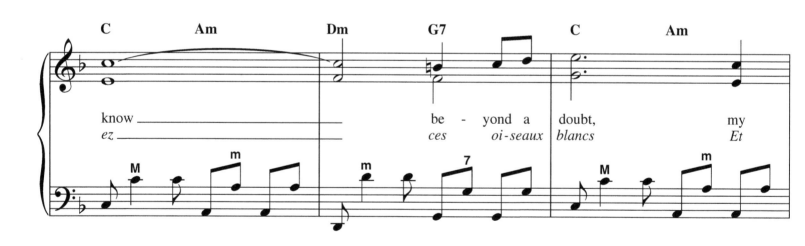

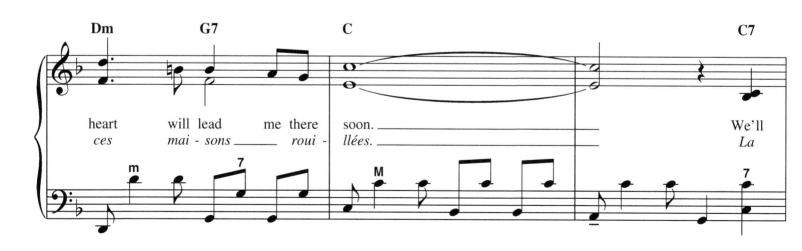

# I LOVE PARIS

**from CAN-CAN**
**from HIGH SOCIETY**

Words and Music by
COLE PORTER

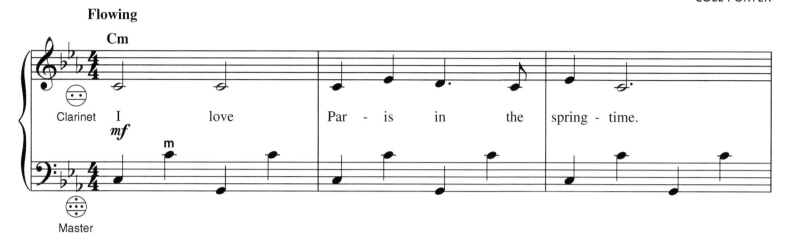

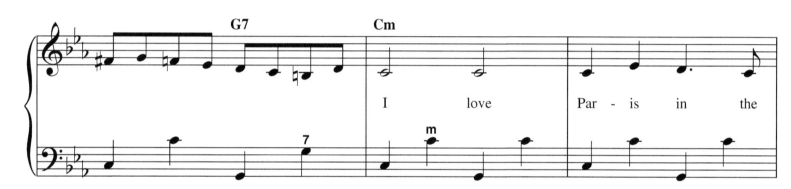

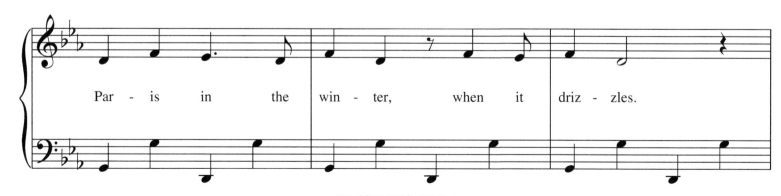

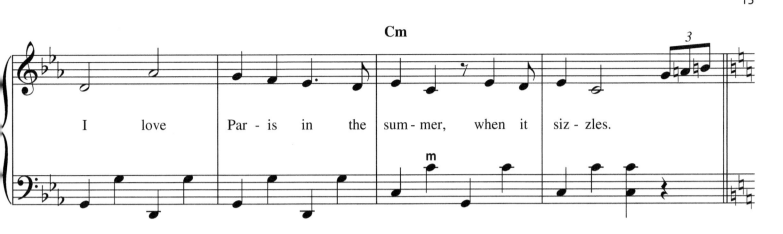

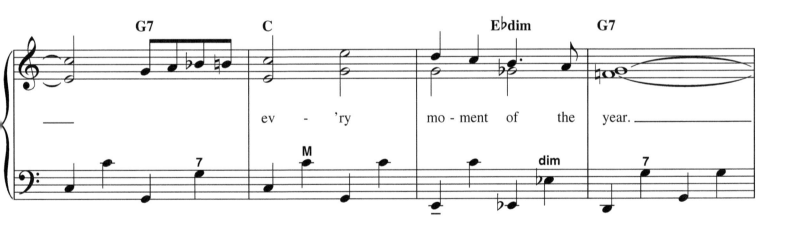

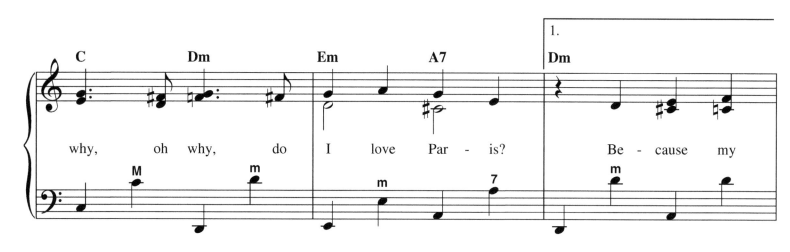

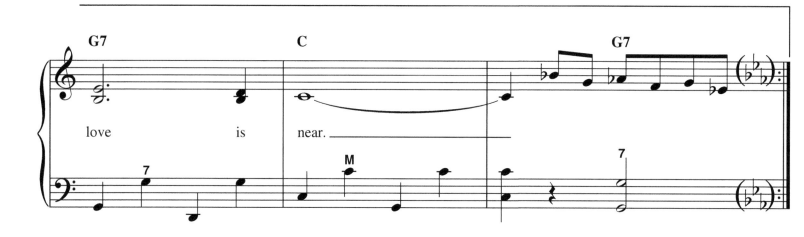

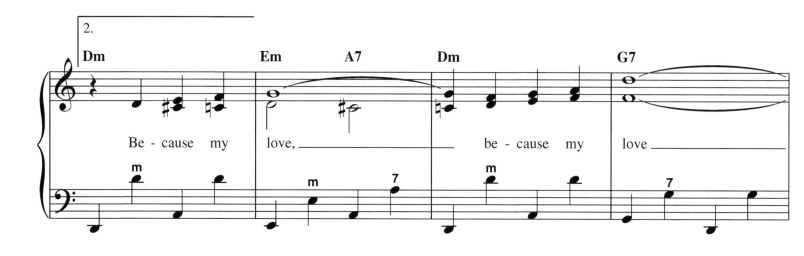

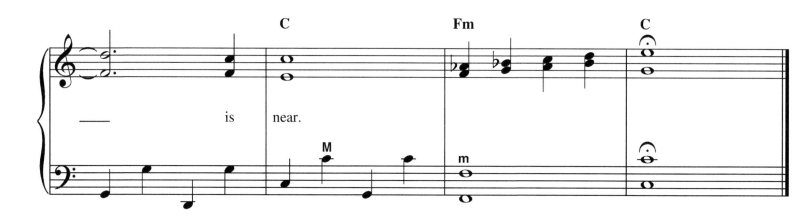

# I WILL WAIT FOR YOU

## from THE UMBRELLAS OF CHERBOURG

Music by MICHEL LEGRAND
Original French Text by JACQUES DEMY
English Words by NORMAN GIMBEL

**Moderately, with a lilt**

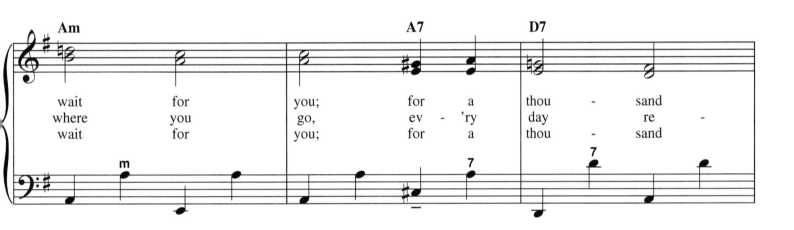

back be - side me, 'til I'm hold - ing
heart be - lieve what in my heart I
here be - side me, 'til I'm touch - ing

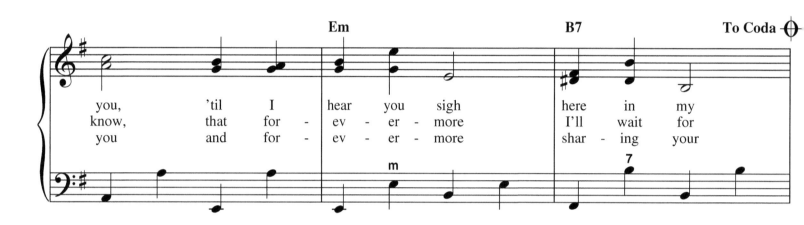

you, 'til I hear you sigh here in my
know, that for - ev - er - more I'll wait my for
you and for - ev - er - more shar - ing your

arms.
An - y
you.

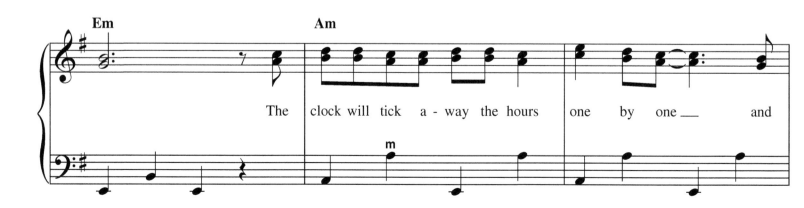

The clock will tick a - way the hours one by one ___ and

then the time will come when all the wait - ing's done, \_\_\_\_ the

time when you re - turn and find me here and run \_\_\_ straight _____

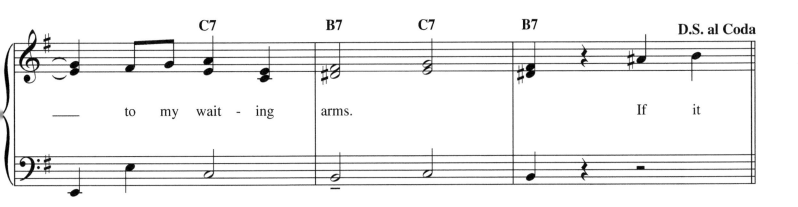

\_\_\_ to my wait - ing arms. If it

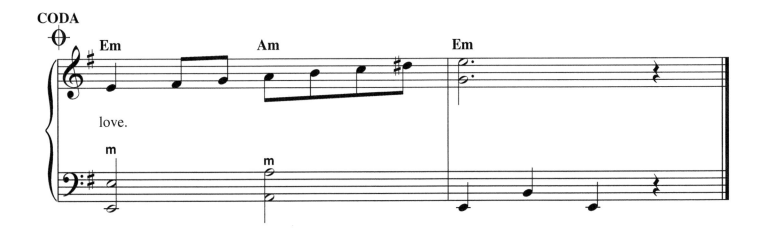

love.

# LA MARSEILLAISE

Words and Music by
CLAUDE ROUGET DE LISLE

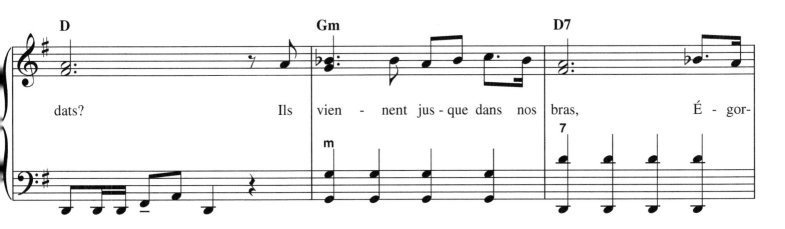

dats? Ils vien - nent jus - que dans nos bras, É - gor-

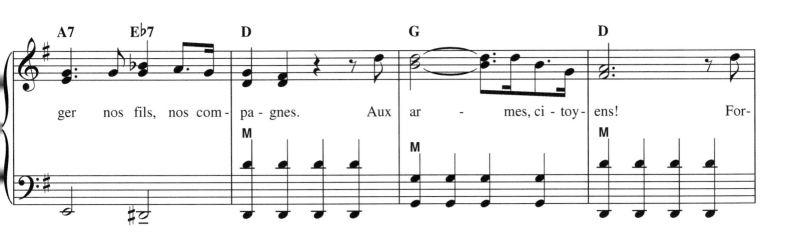

ger nos fils, nos com - pa - gnes. Aux ar - mes, ci - toy - ens! For-

mez _____ vos ba - tail - lons! Mar - chons, mar - chons!

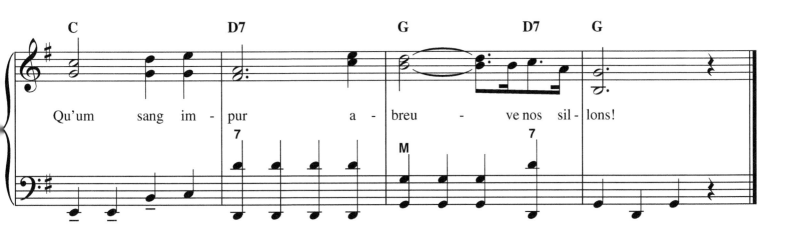

Qu'um sang im - pur a - breu - ve nos sil - lons!

# LET IT BE ME
## (Je T'appartiens)

English Words by MANN CURTIS
French Words by PIERRE DeLANOE
Music by GILBERT BECAUD

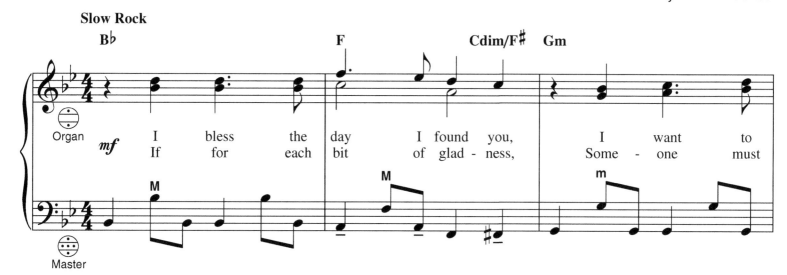

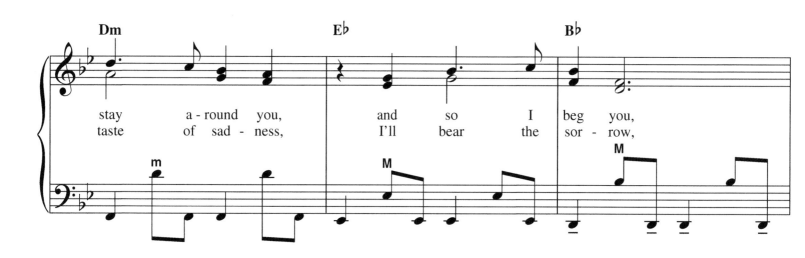

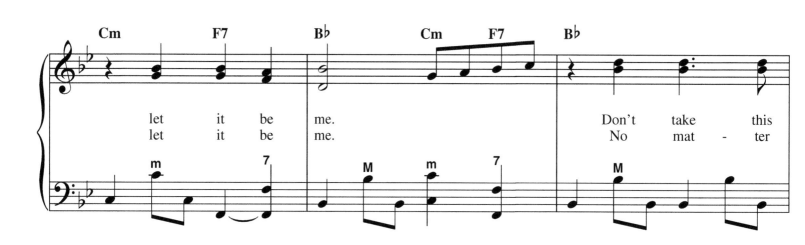

# A MAN AND A WOMAN
## (Un Homme et une Femme)
### from A MAN AND A WOMAN

Original Words by PIERRE BAROUH
English Words by JERRY KELLER
Music by FRANCIS LAI

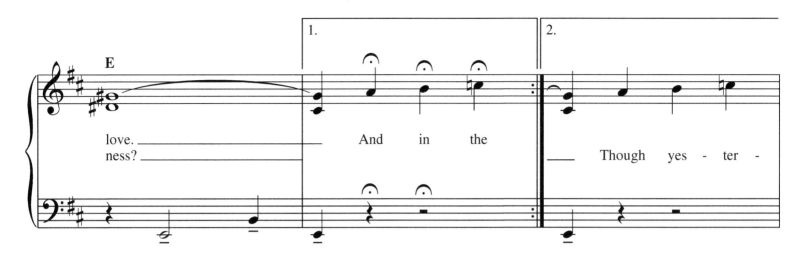

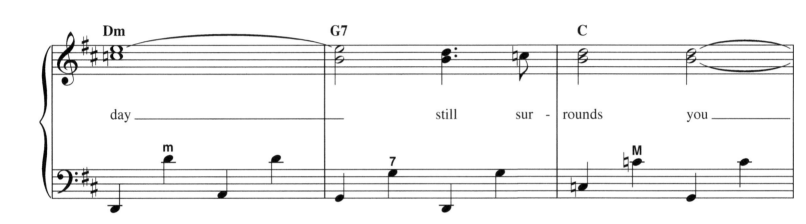

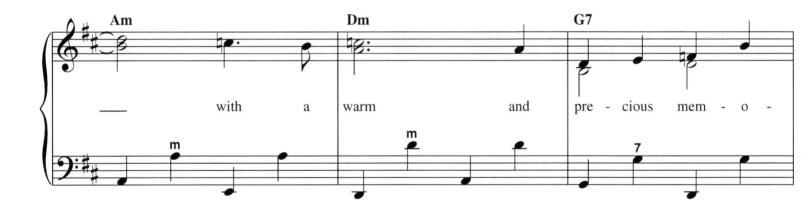

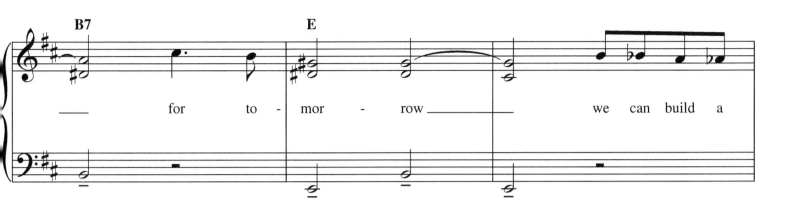

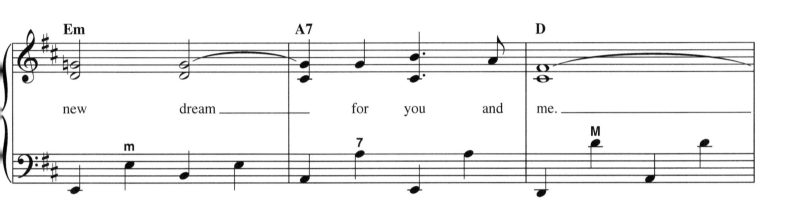

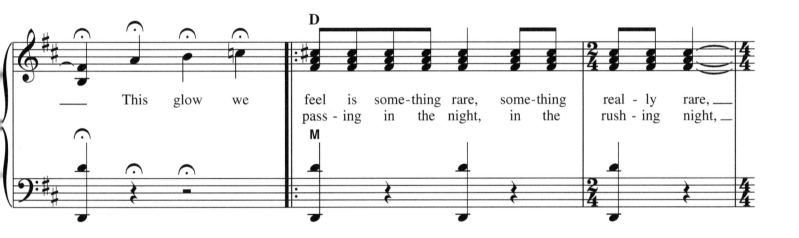

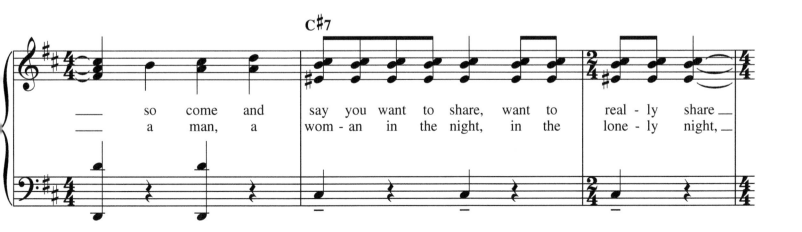

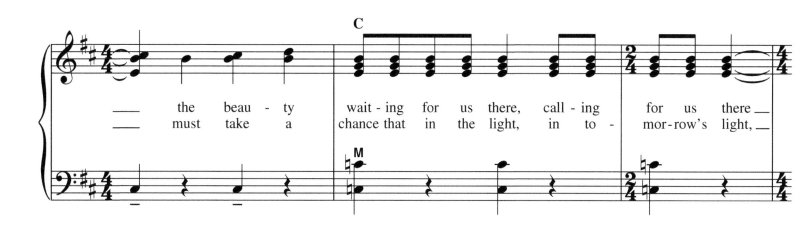

the beau - ty    wait - ing for us there, call - ing    for us there _____
must take  a    chance that in the light, in to - mor-row's light, _____

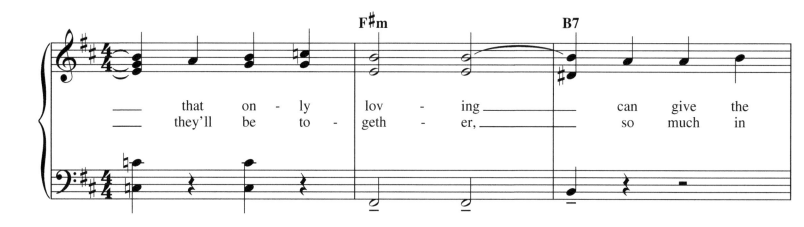

that on - ly    lov - ing _____    can give the
they'll be to - geth - er, _____    so much in

1.

heart. _____    When life is

2.

love. _____

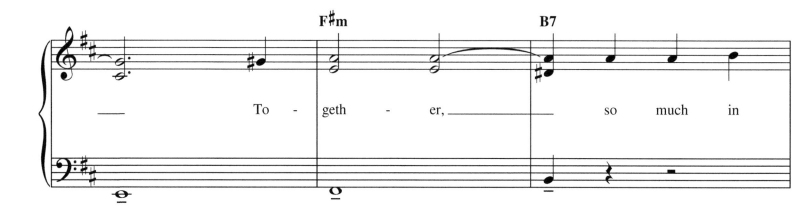

_____ To - geth - er, _____    so much in

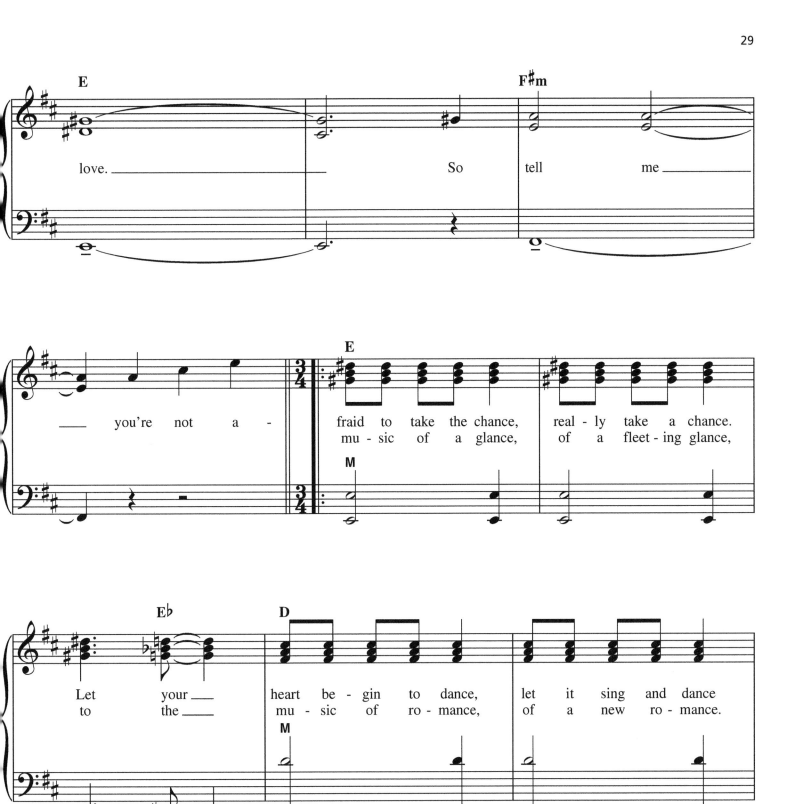

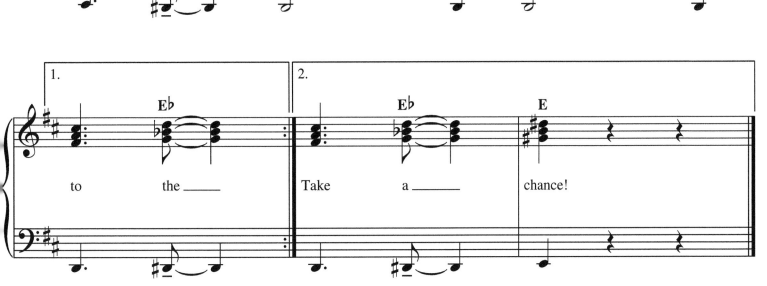

E
F♯m
love. So tell me
you're not a -
E
M
fraid to take the chance, real - ly take a chance.
mu - sic of a glance, of a fleet - ing glance,
E♭
D
M
Let your heart be - gin to dance, let it sing and dance
to the mu - sic of ro - mance, of a new ro - mance.
1.
2.
E♭
E♭
E
to the
Take a chance!

# MY MAN
## (Mon Homme)
### from ZIEGFELD FOLLIES

Words by ALBERT WILLEMETZ and JACQUES CHARLES
English Words by CHANNING POLLOCK
Music by MAURICE YVAIN

**Moderately**

Bandoneon It's cost me a lot, but there's one thing that I've got, it's my man, ___
*Sur cet - te terr', ma seul' joie, mon seul bon-heur c'est mon hom - me*

Master

cold and wet, tired, you bet, but all that I soon for-get with my
*J'ai don - ne' tout c'que j'ai, mon a - mour et tout mon cœur, a mon*

man. ___ He's not much for looks, and no
*hom - me,* *Et mê - me la nuit quand je*

he - ro out of books is my man. ___ Two or
*rè - ve c'est de lui de mon hom - me.* *Ce n'est*

three girls has he that he | likes as well as me, but I | love him! I
pas qu'il est beau qu'il est | ri - che ni cos - taud mais je | l'ai - me, c'est i-

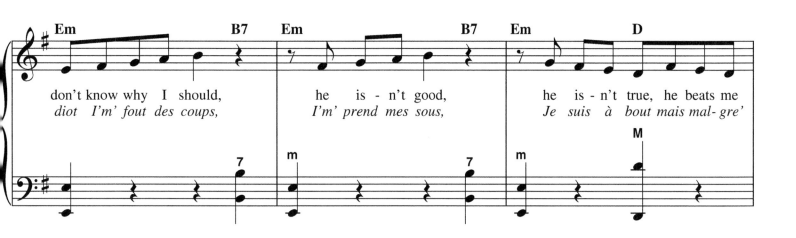

don't know why I should, | he is - n't good, | he is - n't true, he beats me
diot I'm' fout des coups, | I'm' prend mes sous, | Je suis à bout mais mal - gre'

too. What can I do? | Oh, my man, I love him | so, he'll nev - er
tout que vou - lez - vous. | Je l'ai tell' ment dans la | peau qu'j'en d'viens mar -

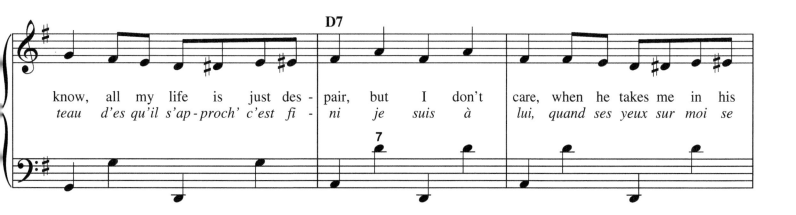

know, all my life is just des - | pair, but I don't | care, when he takes me in his
teau d'es qu'il s'ap - proch' c'est fi - | ni je suis à | lui, quand ses yeux sur moi se

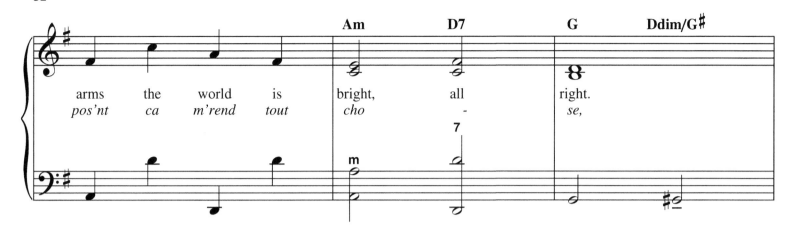

arms the world is bright, all right.
*pos'nt ca m'rend tout cho - se,*

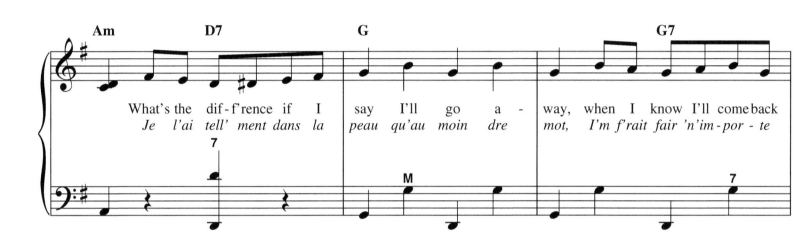

What's the dif-f'rence if I say I'll go a - way, when I know I'll come back
*Je l'ai tell' ment dans la peau qu'au moin dre mot, I'm f'rait fair 'n'im-por-te*

on my knees some - day? For what-ev-er my man is I am his for-
*quoi. J'tue-rais ma foi, j'sens qu'il me rend-rait in - fâme, mais je n'suis qu'un'*

ev - er - more! Oh, my man, I love him
*fem - me. Et j'lai tell' ment dans la*

# LA PETIT VALSE
## (The Petite Waltz)

English Lyric by E.A. ELLINGTON
and PHYLLIS CLAIRE
Music by JOE HEYNE

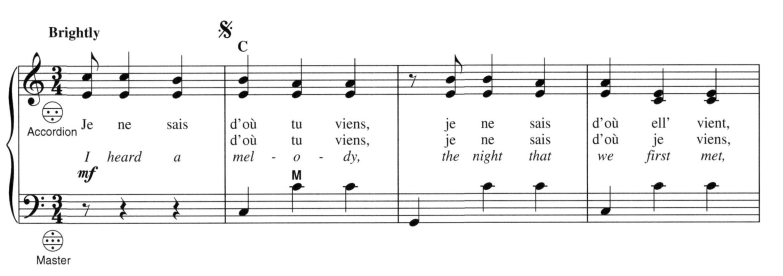

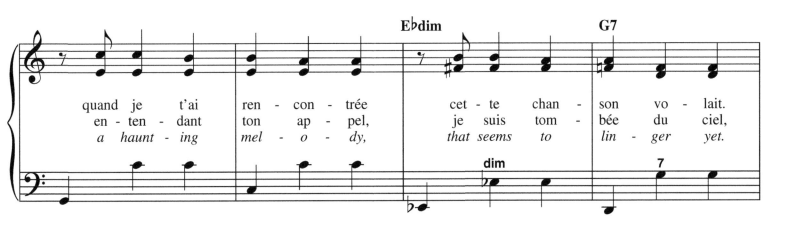

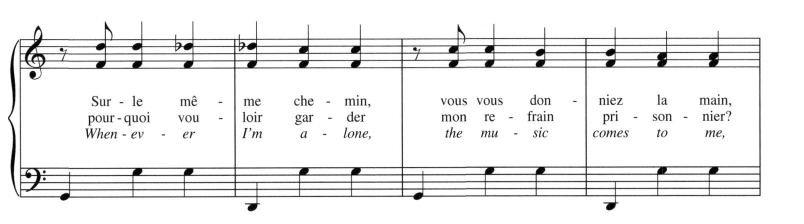

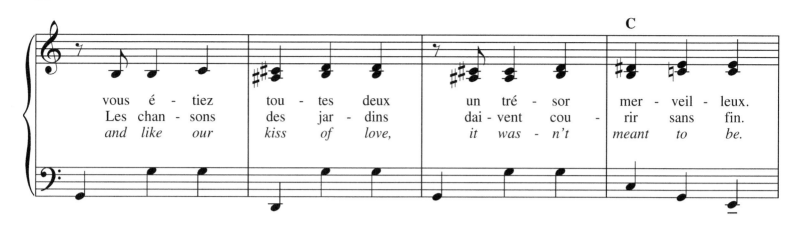

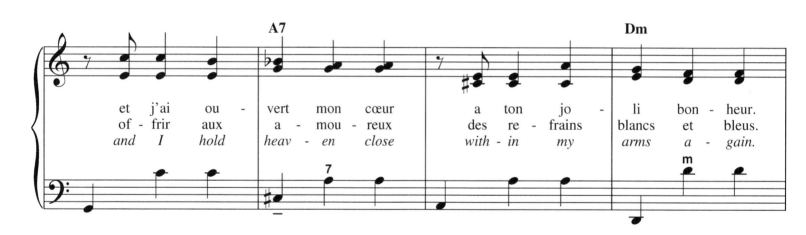

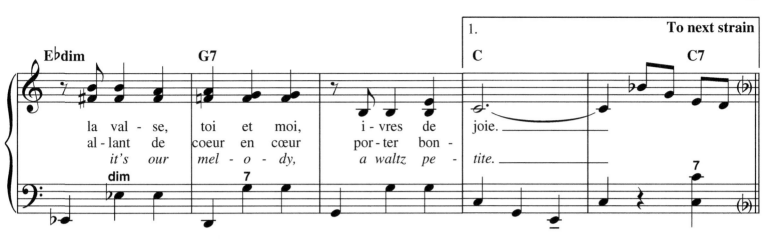

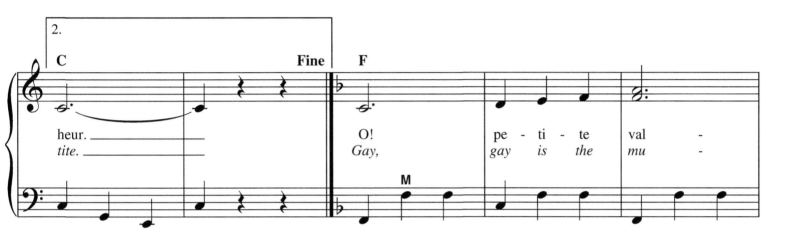

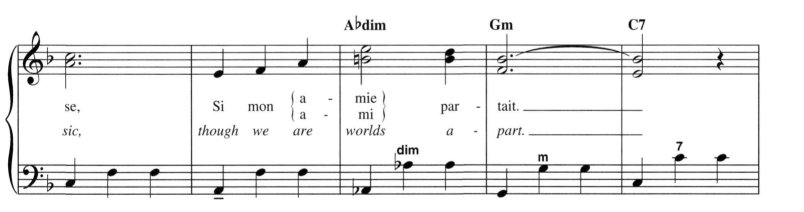

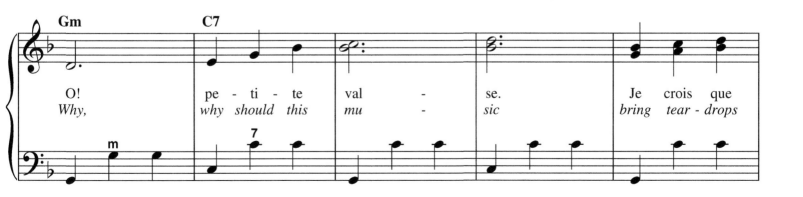

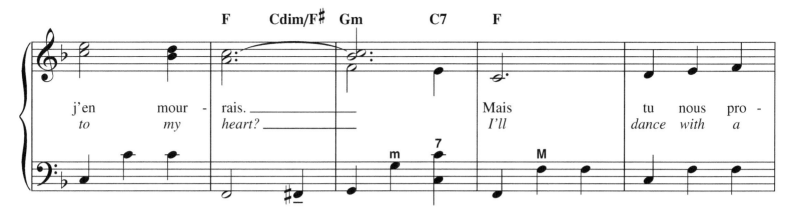

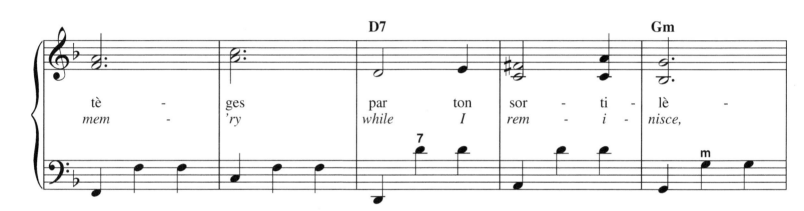

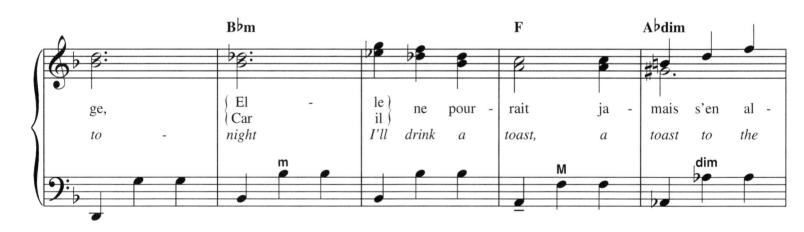

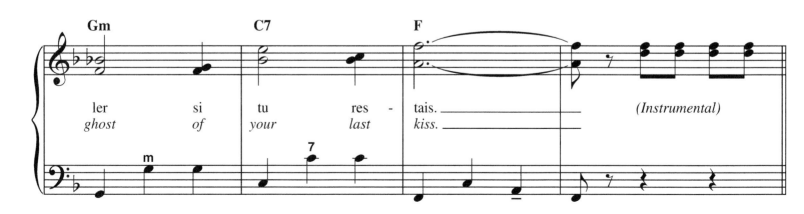

(Instrumental)

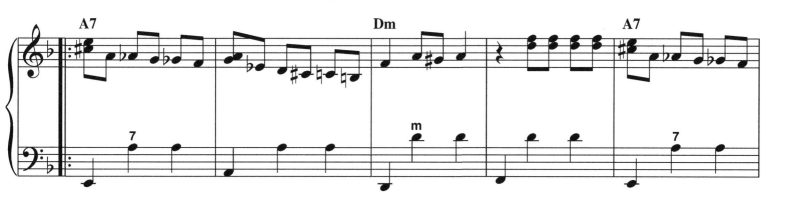

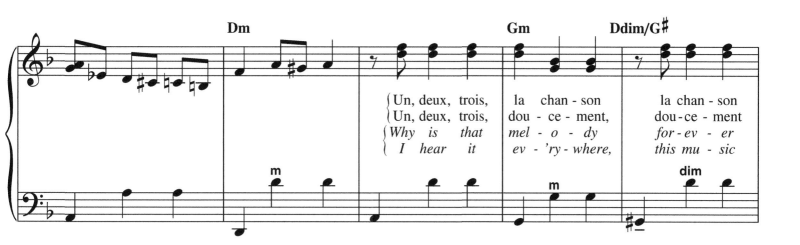

Un, deux, trois, | la chan - son | la chan - son
Un, deux, trois, | dou - ce - ment, | dou - ce - ment
*Why is that* | *mel - o - dy* | *for - ev - er*
*I hear it* | *ev - 'ry - where,* | *this mu - sic*

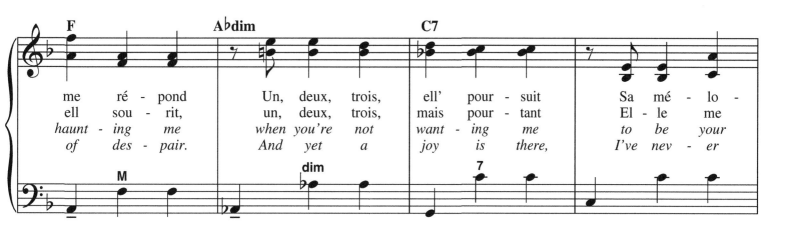

me ré - pond | Un, deux, trois, | ell' pour - suit | Sa mé - lo -
ell sou - rit, | un, deux, trois, | mais pour - tant | El - le me
*haunt - ing me* | *when you're not* | *want - ing me* | *to be your*
*of des - pair.* | *And yet a* | *joy is there,* | *I've nev - er*

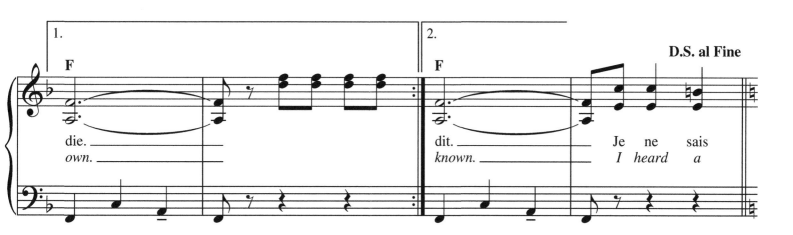

**1.**

die. ____
*own.* ____

**2.**

**D.S. al Fine**

dit. ____ Je ne sais
*known.* ____ *I heard a*

# PIGALLE

English Lyric by CHARLES NEWMAN
French Lyric by GEO KOGER,
GEORGES ULMER and GUY LUYPAERTS
Music by GEORGES ULMER and GUY LUYPAERTS

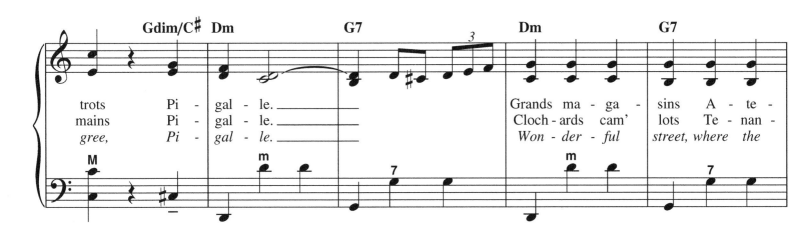

Un p'tit jet d'eau Un' sta - tion de mé - tro En - tou - rée de bis -
Girls et mann' - quins Gi - tans aux yeux ma - lins Qui li - sent dans les
*What makes Par - ee like Par - ee ought to be? All the na - tives a -*

trots Pi - gal - le. _____ Grands ma - ga - sins A - te -
mains Pi - gal - le. _____ Cloch - ards cam' lots Te - nan -
*gree, Pi - gal - le. _____ Won - der - ful street, where the*

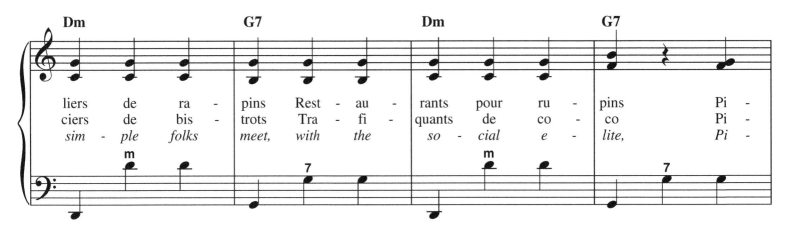

liers de ra - pins Rest - au - rants pour ru - pins Pi -
ciers de bis - trots Tra - fi - quants de co - co Pi -
*sim - ple folks meet, with the so - cial e - lite, Pi -*

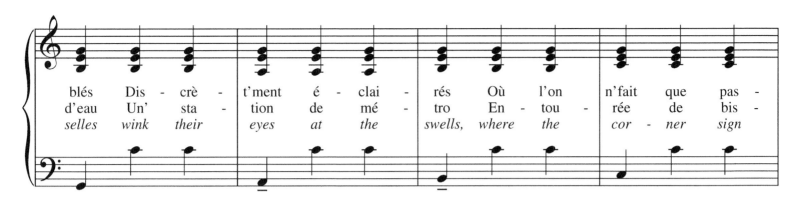

blés Dis - crè - t'ment é - clai - rés Où l'on n'fait que pas -
d'eau Un' sta - tion de mé - tro En - tou - rée de bis -
*selles wink their eyes at the swells, where the cor - ner sign*

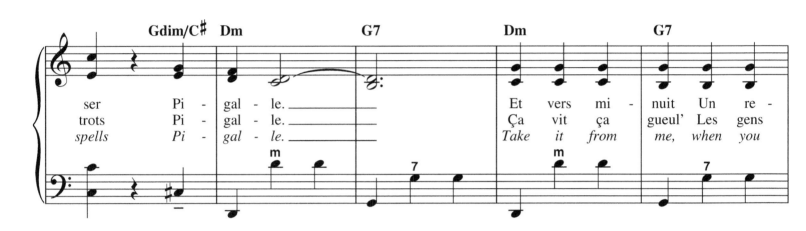

ser Pi - gal - le. Et vers mi - nuit Un re -
trots Pi - gal - le. Ça vit ça gueul' Les gens
*spells Pi - gal - le. Take it from me, when you*

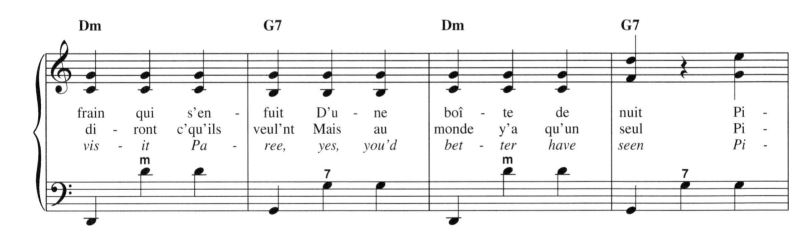

frain qui s'en - fuit D'u - ne boî - te de nuit Pi -
di - ront c'qu'ils veul'nt Mais au monde y'a qu'un seul Pi -
*vis - it Pa - ree, yes, you'd bet - ter have seen Pi -*

gal - le.
gal - le.
*gal - le.*

gal - le.
gal - le.
*gal - le.*

# QUE RESTE-T-IL DE NOS AMOURS

## (I Wish You Love)

Words and Music by
CHARLES TRENET
English Lyric by ALBERT BEACH

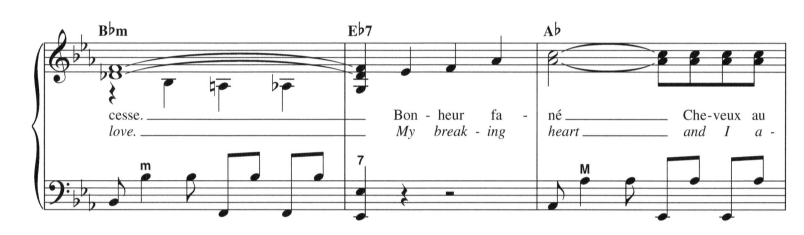

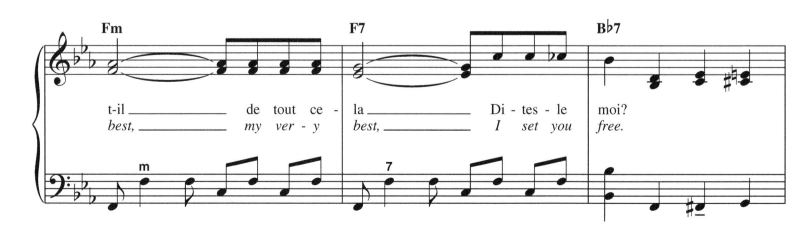

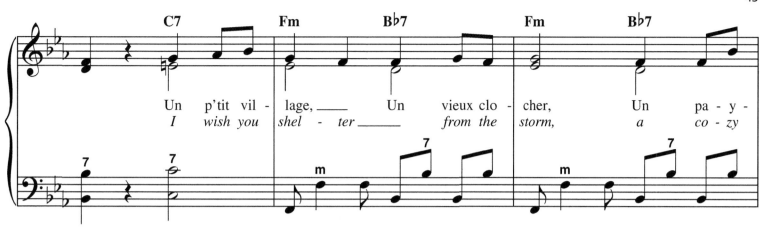
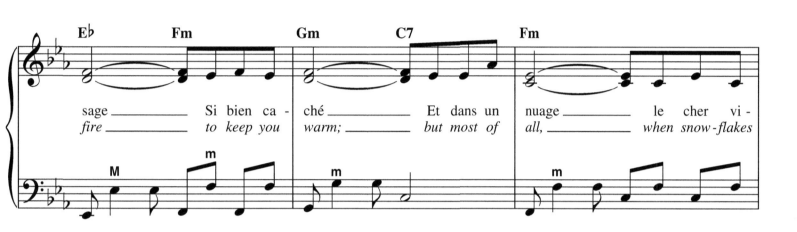
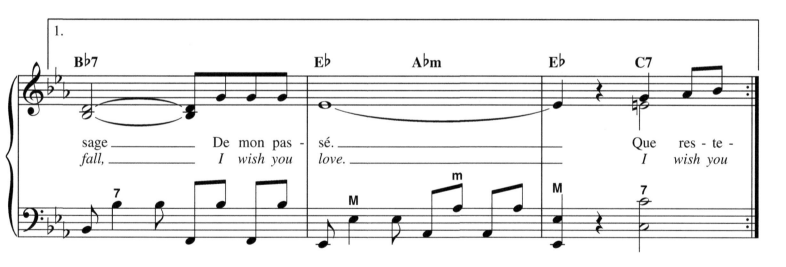
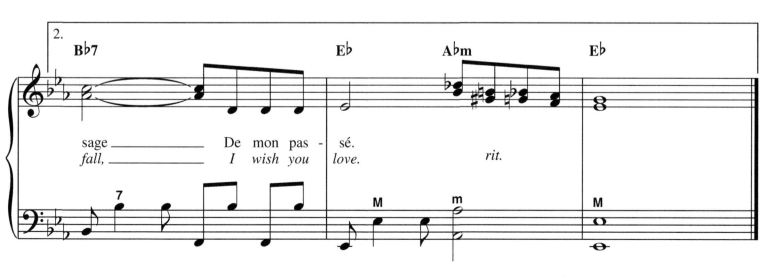

# THE POOR PEOPLE OF PARIS
## (Jean's Song)

Original French words by RENE ROUZAUD
English words by JACK LAWRENCE
Music by MARGUERITE MONNOT

**Moderately, with spirit**

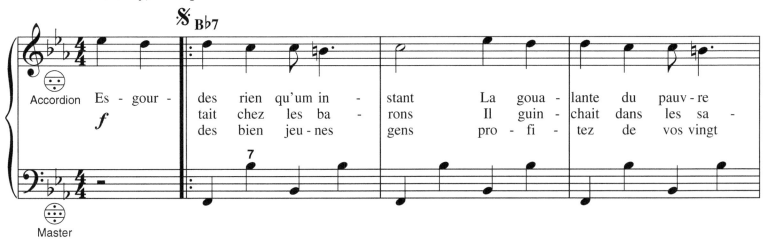

Es - gour- | des rien qu'um in - | stant La goua - lante du pauv - re
tait chez les ba - | rons Il guin - chait dans les sa -
des bien jeu - nes | gens pro - fi - | tez de vos vingt

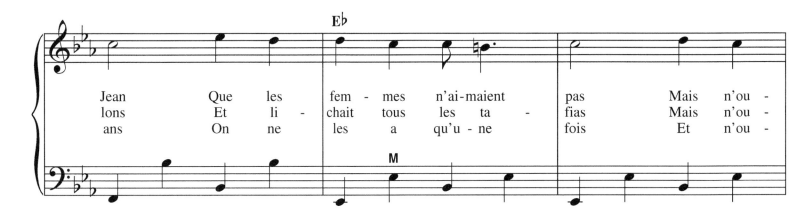

Jean Que les | fem - mes n'ai-maient | pas Mais n'ou -
lons Et li - | chait tous les ta - | fias Mais n'ou -
ans On ne | les a qu'u - ne | fois Et n'ou -

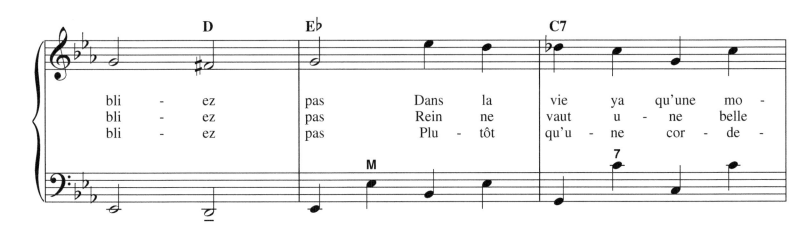

bli - ez | pas Dans la vie ya qu'une mo -
bli - ez | pas Rein ne vaut u - ne belle
bli - ez | pas Plu - tôt qu'u - ne cor - de -

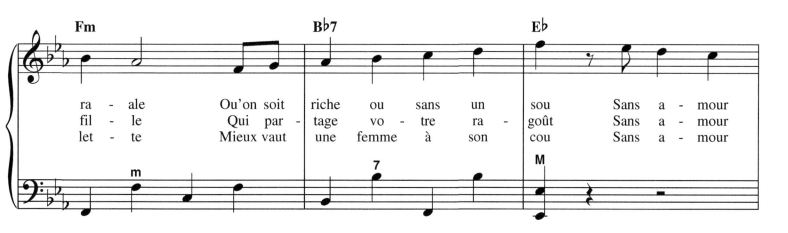

ra - ale    Ou'on soit    riche    ou    sans    un    sou    Sans  a - mour
fil - le    Qui par - tage    vo - tre    ra -    goût    Sans  a - mour
let - te    Mieux vaut    une    femme    à    son    cou    Sans  a - mour

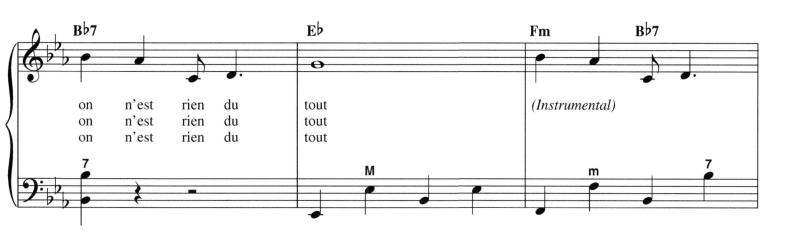

on    n'est    rien    du    tout    (Instrumental)
on    n'est    rien    du    tout
on    n'est    rien    du    tout

To Coda

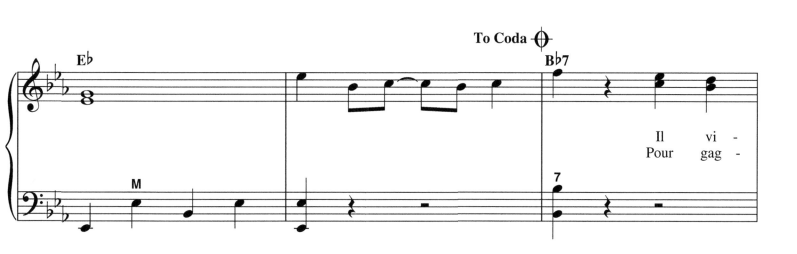

Il    vi -
Pour    gag -

vait    au    jour    le    jour    Dans    la    soie    et    le    ve -
ner    des    pi - cail -    lons    Il    fut    un    mé - chant    lar -

46

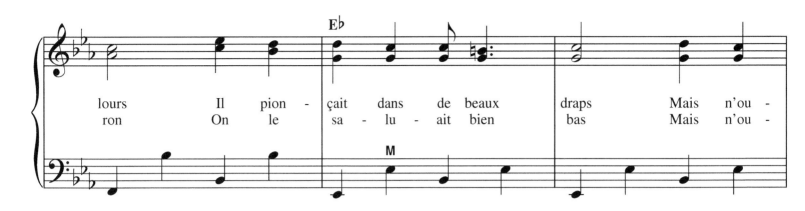

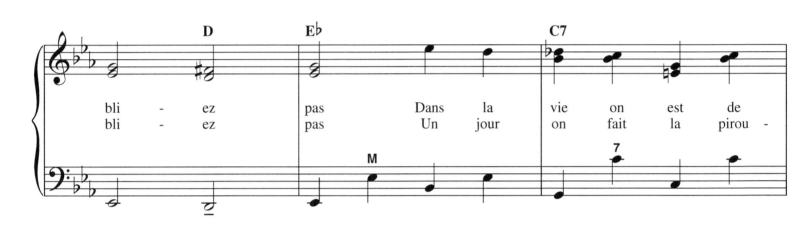

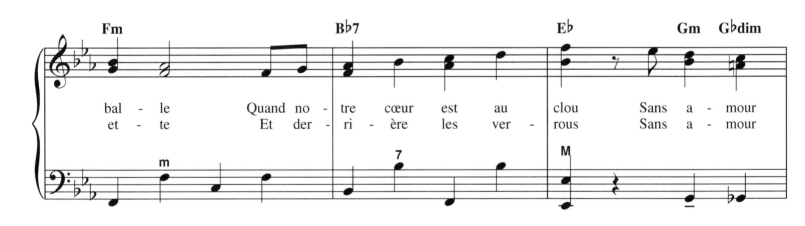

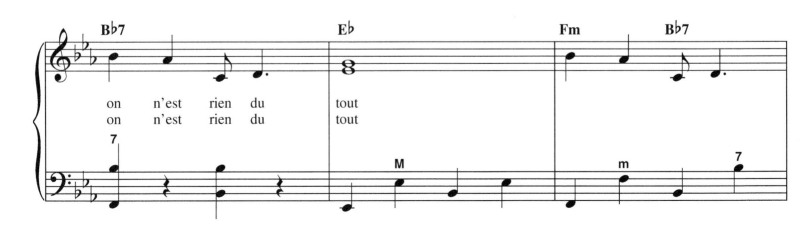

# SOUS LE CIEL DE PARIS
## (Under Paris Skies)

English Words by KIM GANNON
French Words by JEAN DREJAC
Music by HUBERT GIRAUD

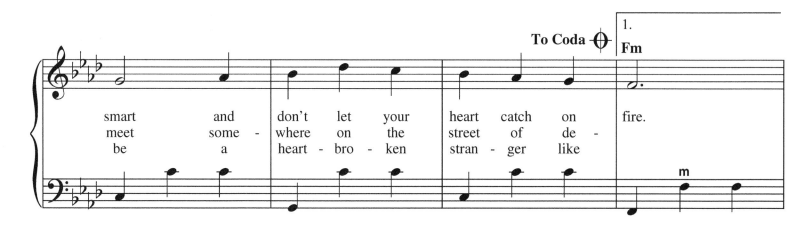

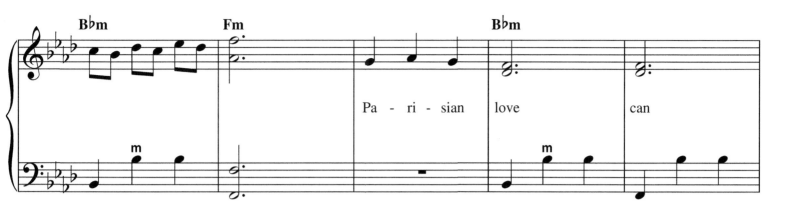

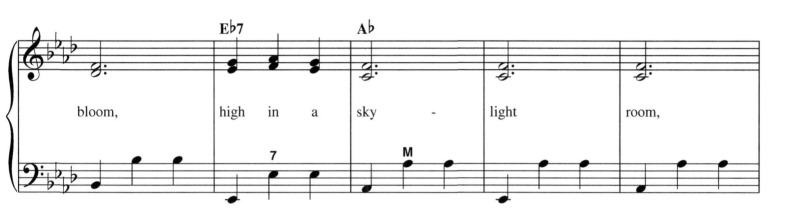

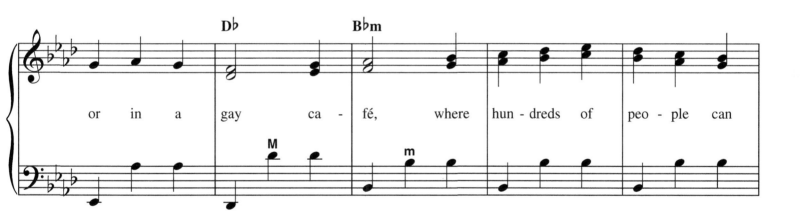

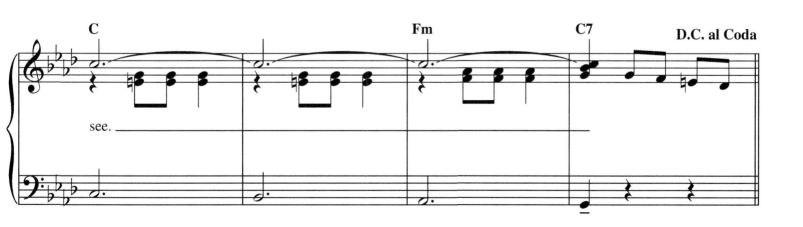

**CODA**

me. _____ Oh, I fell in

love, _____ yes, I was a

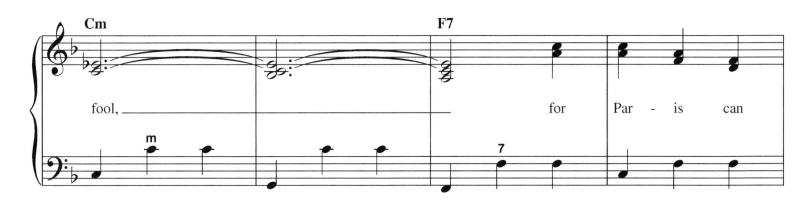

fool, _____ for Par - is can

be _____ so beau - ti - f'lly

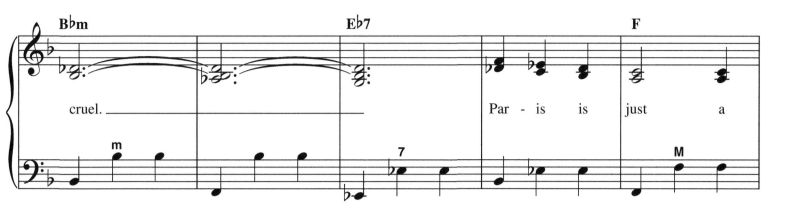

cruel. _____ Par - is is just a

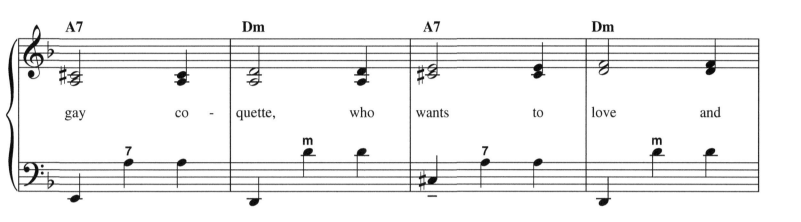

gay co - quette, who wants to love and

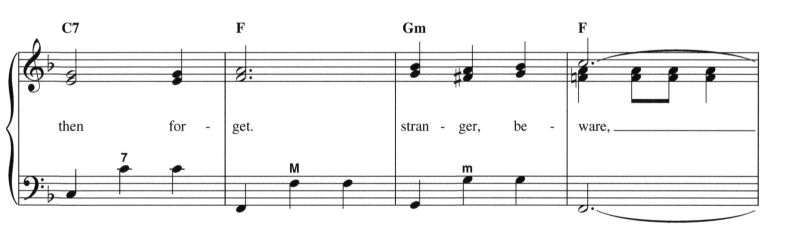

then for - get. stran - ger, be - ware, _____

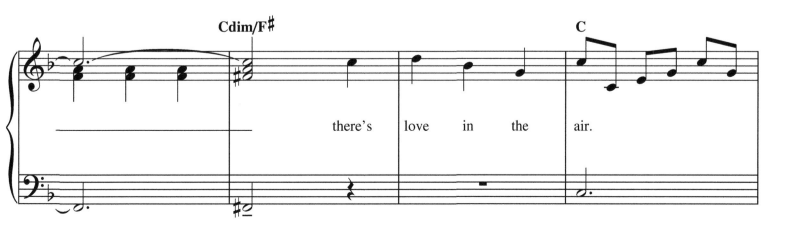

_____ there's love in the air.

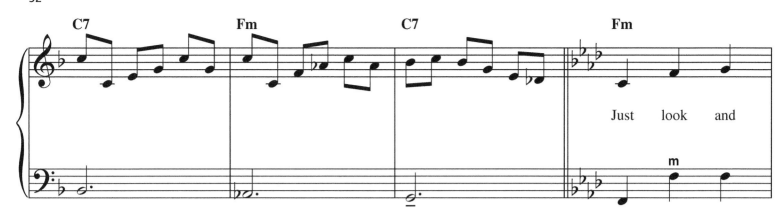

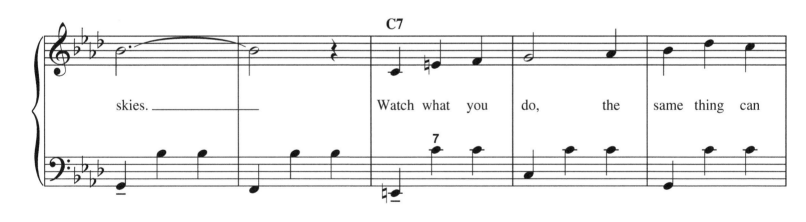

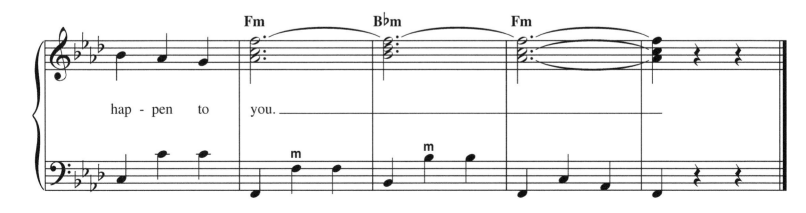

# WATCH WHAT HAPPENS
## from THE UMBRELLAS OF CHERBOURG

Music by MICHEL LEGRAND
Original French Text by JACQUES DEMY
English Words by NORMAN GIMBEL

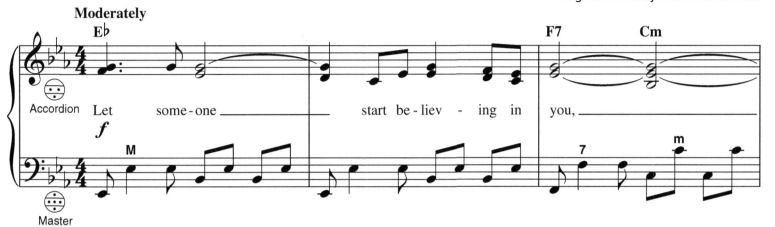

Let some-one _____ start be-liev-ing in you, _____

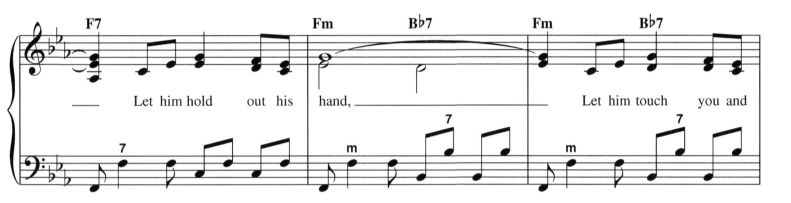

_____ Let him hold out his hand, _____ Let him touch you and

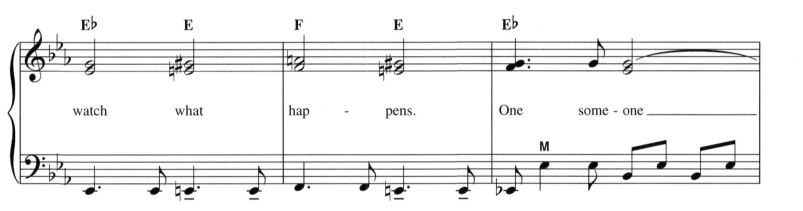

watch what hap - pens. One some - one _____

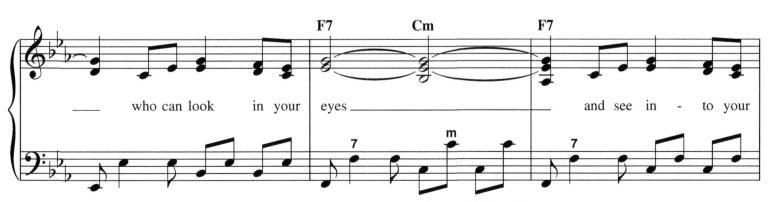

_____ who can look in your eyes _____ and see in - to your

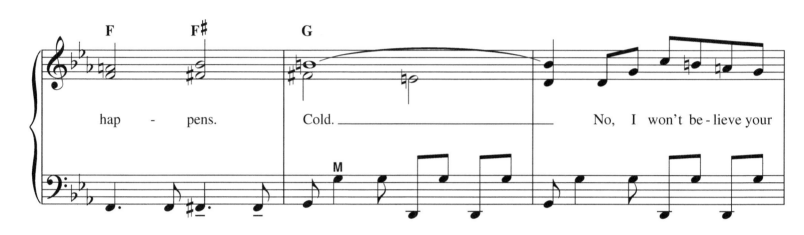

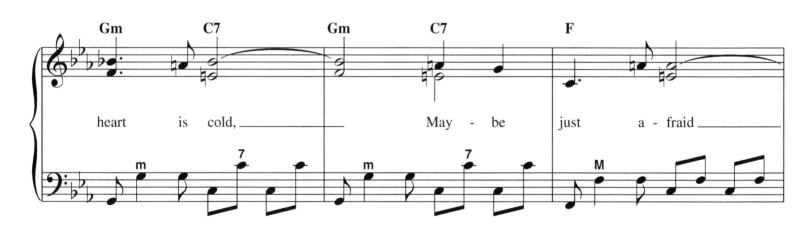

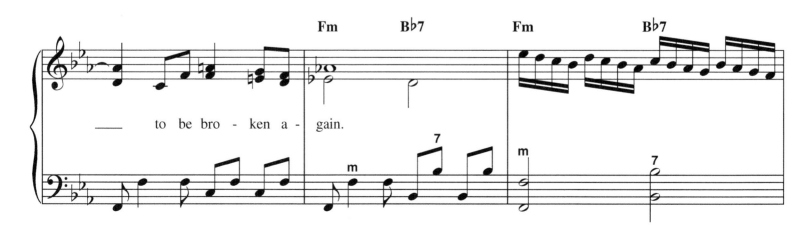

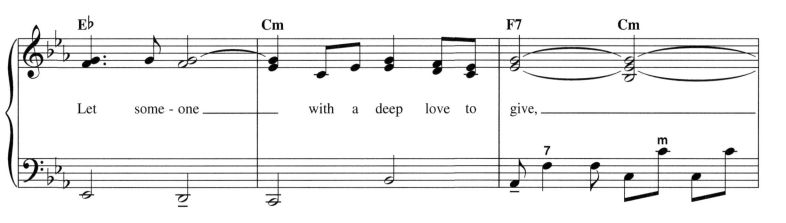

Let some-one _____ with a deep love to give, _____

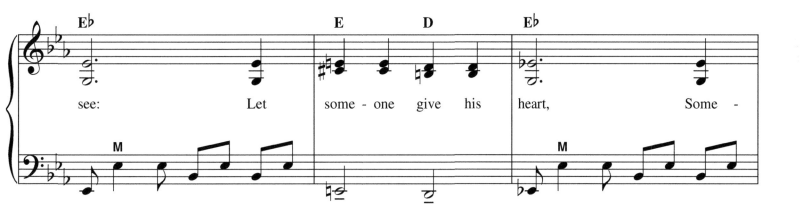

_____ Give that deep love to you _____ and what mag - ic you'll

see: Let some - one give his heart, Some -

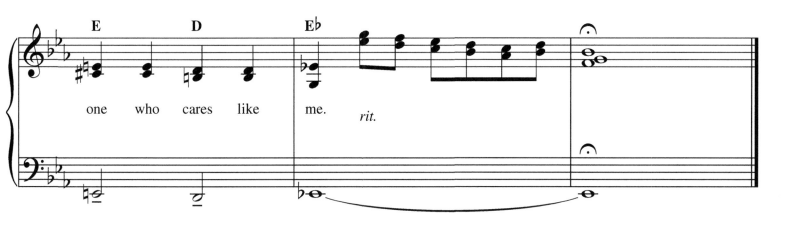

one who cares like me. *rit.*

# ET MAINTENANT
## (What Now, My Love)

Original French Lyric by PIERRE DELANO
Music by FRANCOIS BECAUD
English Adaptation by CARL SIGMAN

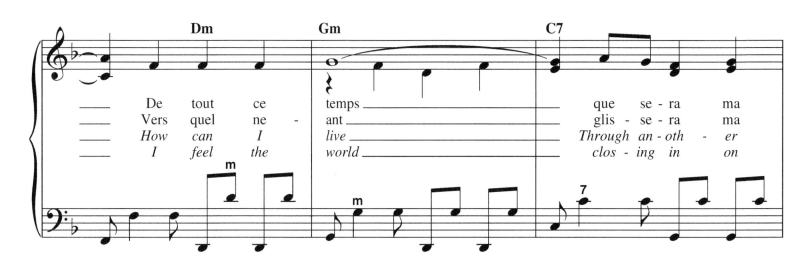

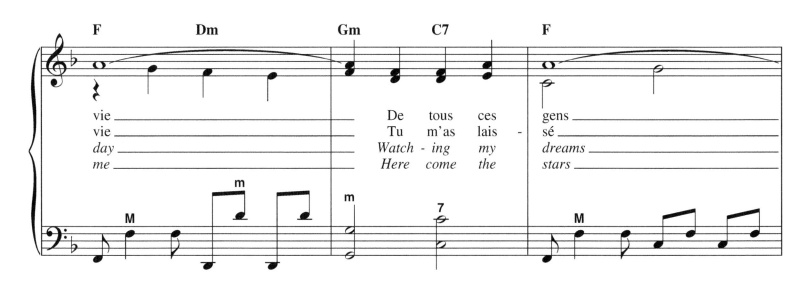

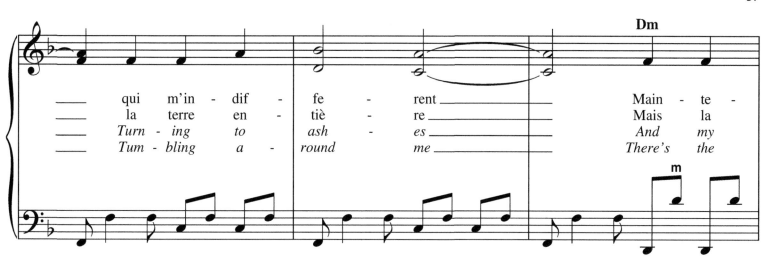

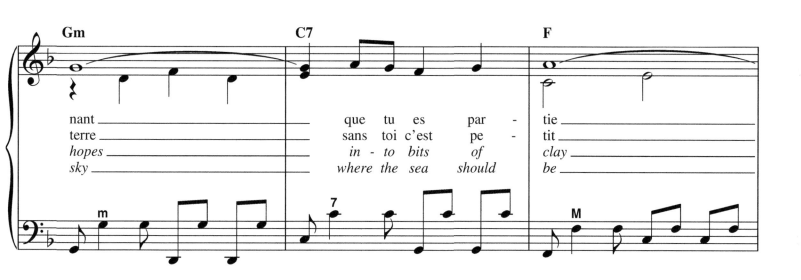

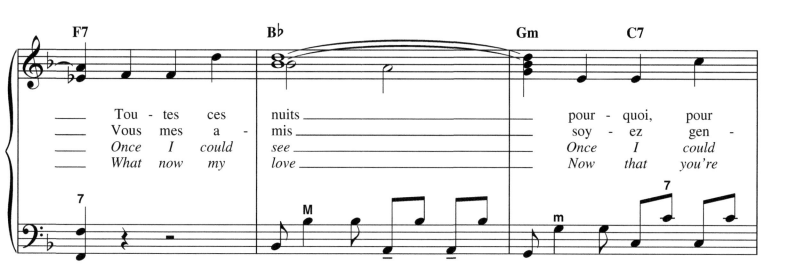

# WHERE IS YOUR HEART
## (The Song from Moulin Rouge)

Words by WILLIAM ENGVICK
Music by GEORGE AURIC

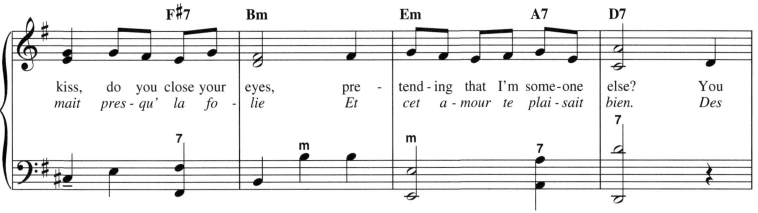

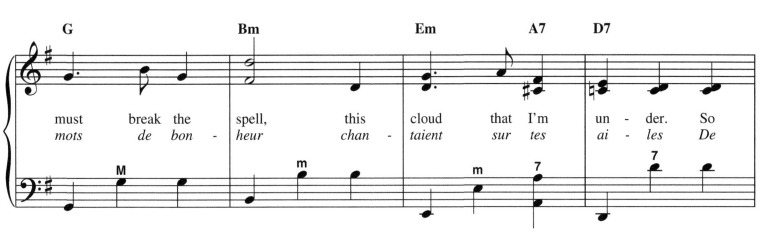

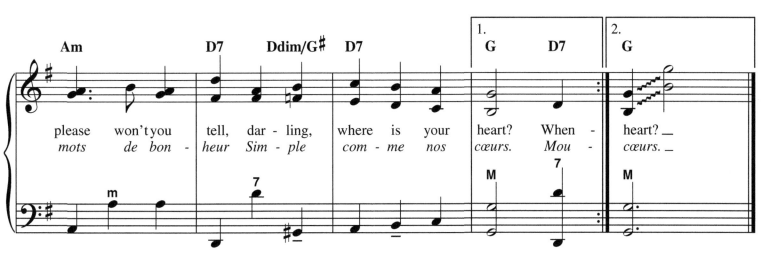

# A COLLECTION OF ALL-TIME FAVORITES
## FOR ACCORDION

### ACCORDION FAVORITES
*arr. Gary Meisner*

16 all-time favorites, arranged for accordion, including: Can't Smile Without You • Could I Have This Dance • Endless Love • Memory • Sunrise, Sunset • I.O.U. • and more.
00359012................................................$12.99

### ALL-TIME FAVORITES FOR ACCORDION
*arr. Gary Meisner*

20 must-know standards arranged for accordions. Includes: Ain't Misbehavin' • Autumn Leaves • Crazy • Hello, Dolly! • Hey, Good Lookin' • Moon River • Speak Softly, Love • Unchained Melody • The Way We Were • Zip-A-Dee-Doo-Dah • and more.
00311088................................................$12.99

### THE BEATLES FOR ACCORDION

17 hits from the Lads from Liverpool have been arranged for accordion. Includes: All You Need Is Love • Eleanor Rigby • The Fool on the Hill • Here Comes the Sun • Hey Jude • In My Life • Let It Be • Ob-La-Di, Ob-La-Da • Penny Lane • When I'm Sixty-Four • Yesterday • and more.
00268724 ...............................................$14.99

### BROADWAY FAVORITES
*arr. Ken Kotwitz*

A collection of 17 wonderful show songs, including: Don't Cry for Me Argentina • Getting to Know You • If I Were a Rich Man • Oklahoma • People Will Say We're in Love • We Kiss in a Shadow.
00490157................................................$10.99

### DISNEY SONGS FOR ACCORDION – 3RD EDITION

13 Disney favorites especially arranged for accordion, including: Be Our Guest • Beauty and the Beast • Can You Feel the Love Tonight • Chim Chim Cher-ee • It's a Small World • Let It Go • Under the Sea • A Whole New World • You'll Be in My Heart • Zip-A-Dee-Doo-Dah • and more!
00152508 ...............................................$12.99

### FIRST 50 SONGS YOU SHOULD PLAY ON THE ACCORDION
*arr. Gary Meisner*

If you're new to the accordion, you are probably eager to learn some songs. This book provides 50 simplified arrangements of must-know popular standards, folk songs and show tunes, including: All of Me • Beer Barrel Polka • Carnival of Venice • Edelweiss • Hava Nagila (Let's Be Happy) • Hernando's Hideaway • Jambalaya (On the Bayou) • Lady of Spain • Moon River • 'O Sole Mio • Sentimental Journey • Somewhere, My Love • That's Amore (That's Love) • Under Paris Skies • and more. Includes lyrics when applicable.
00250269 .............................................$16.99

### FRENCH SONGS FOR ACCORDION
*arr. Gary Meisner*

A très magnifique collection of 17 French standards arranged for the accordion. Includes: Autumn Leaves • Beyond the Sea • C'est Magnifique • I Love Paris • La Marseillaise • Let It Be Me (Je T'appartiens) • Under Paris Skies • Watch What Happens • and more.
00311498................................................$10.99

### HYMNS FOR ACCORDION
*arr. Gary Meisner*

24 treasured sacred favorites arranged for accordion, including: Amazing Grace • Beautiful Savior • Come, Thou Fount of Every Blessing • Crown Him with Many Crowns • Holy, Holy, Holy • It Is Well with My Soul • Just a Closer Walk with Thee • A Mighty Fortress Is Our God • Nearer, My God, to Thee • The Old Rugged Cross • Rock of Ages • What a Friend We Have in Jesus • and more.
00277160 ...............................................$9.99

### ITALIAN SONGS FOR ACCORDION
*arr. Gary Meisner*

17 favorite Italian standards arranged for accordion, including: Carnival of Venice • Ciribiribin • Come Back to Sorrento • Funiculi, Funicula • La donna è mobile • La Spagnola • 'O Sole Mio • Santa Lucia • Tarantella • and more.
00311089................................................$12.99

### LATIN FAVORITES FOR ACCORDION
*arr. Gary Meisner*

20 Latin favorites, including: Bésame Mucho (Kiss Me Much) • The Girl from Ipanema • How Insensitive (Insensatez) • Perfidia • Spanish Eyes • So Nice (Summer Samba) • and more.
00310932................................................$14.99

### THE FRANK MAROCCO ACCORDION SONGBOOK

This songbook includes arrangements and recordings of 15 standards and original songs from legendary jazz accordionist Frank Marocco, including: All the Things You Are • Autumn Leaves • Beyond the Sea • Moon River • Moonlight in Vermont • Stormy Weather (Keeps Rainin' All the Time) • and more!
00233441 Book/Online Audio...............$19.99

### POP STANDARDS FOR ACCORDION
*Arrangements of 20 Classic Songs*

20 classic pop standards arranged for accordion are included in this collection: Annie's Song • Chances Are • For Once in My Life • Help Me Make It Through the Night • My Cherie Amour • Ramblin' Rose • (Sittin' On) The Dock of the Bay • That's Amore (That's Love) • Unchained Melody • and more.
00254822 ...............................................$14.99

### POLKA FAVORITES
*arr. Kenny Kotwitz*

An exciting new collection of 16 songs, including: Beer Barrel Polka • Liechtensteiner Polka • My Melody of Love • Paloma Blanca • Pennsylvania Polka • Too Fat Polka • and more.
00311573................................................$12.99

### STAR WARS FOR ACCORDION

A dozen songs from the Star Wars franchise: The Imperial March (Darth Vader's Theme) • Luke and Leia • March of the Resistance • Princess Leia's Theme • Rey's Theme • Star Wars (Main Theme) • and more.
00157380 ...............................................$14.99

### TANGOS FOR ACCORDION
*arr. Gary Meisner*

Every accordionist needs to know some tangos! Here are 15 favorites: Amapola (Pretty Little Poppy) • Aquellos Ojos Verdes (Green Eyes) • Hernando's Hideaway • Jalousie (Jealousy) • Kiss of Fire • La Cumparsita (The Masked One) • Quizás, Quizás, Quizás (Perhaps, Perhaps, Perhaps) • The Rain in Spain • Tango of Roses • Whatever Lola Wants (Lola Gets) • and more!
00122252 ...............................................$12.99

### 3-CHORD SONGS FOR ACCORDION
*arr. Gary Meisner*

Here are nearly 30 songs that are easy to play but still sound great! Includes: Amazing Grace • Can Can • Danny Boy • For He's a Jolly Good Fellow • He's Got the Whole World in His Hands • Just a Closer Walk with Thee • La Paloma Blanca (The White Dove) • My Country, 'Tis of Thee • Ode to Joy • Oh! Susanna • Yankee Doodle • The Yellow Rose of Texas • and more.
00312104 ...........................................$12.99

### LAWRENCE WELK'S POLKA FOLIO

More than 50 famous polkas, schottisches and waltzes arranged for piano and accordion, including: Blue Eyes • Budweiser Polka • Clarinet Polka • Cuckoo Polka • The Dove Polka • Draw One Polka • Gypsy Polka • Helena Polka • International Waltzes • Let's Have Another One • Schnitzelbank • Shuffle Schottische • Squeeze Box Polka • Waldteuful Waltzes • and more.
00123218................................................$14.99

**HAL•LEONARD®**
Visit Hal Leonard Online at
**www.halleonard.com**